Porpoises

By Jodie Shepherd

Children's Press®

An Imprint of Scholastic Inc.

Content Consultant
Becky Ellsworth
Curator, Shores Region
Columbus Zoo and Aquarium

Library of Congress Cataloging-in-Publication Data
Names: Shepherd, Jodie, author.
Title: Porpoises/by Jodie Shepherd.
Other titles: Nature's children (New York, N.Y.)
Description: New York, NY: Children's Press, an imprint of Scholastic Inc., 2018. | Series: Nature's children | Includes index.
Identifiers: LCCN 2017036399| ISBN 9780531234822 (library binding) | ISBN 9780531245125 (pbk.)
Subjects: LCSH: Porpoises—Juvenile literature.
Classification: LCC QL737.C434 S54 2018 | DDC 599.53/9—dc23
LC record available at https://lccn.loc.gov/2017036399

Design by Anna Tunick Tabachnik

Creative Direction: Judith Christ-Lafond for Scholastic

Produced by Spooky Cheetah Press

Printed in North Mankato, MN, USA   113

SCHOLASTIC, CHILDREN'S PRESS, NATURE'S CHILDREN™, and associated logos
are trademarks and/or registered trademarks of Scholastic Inc.

1 2 3 4 5 6 7 8 9 10 R 27 26 25 24 23 22 21 20 19 18

Scholastic Inc., 557 Broadway, New York, NY 10012.

Photos ©: cover: Hiroya Minakuchi/Minden Pictures; 1: Cheng Min Xinhua/eyevine/Redux; 4 leaf silo and throughout:
stockgraphicdesigns.com; 5 porpoise silos and throughout: Loveleen Kaur/123RF; 5 child silo: All-Silhouettes.com; 5 bottom:
Solvin Zankl/Alamy Images; 7: Eddy Joaquim/Getty Images; 8-9: Jelger Herder/Buiten-beeld/Minden Pictures; 11: Solvin Zankl/
NPL/Minden Pictures; 12-13: David Tipling/Getty Images; 15: Seapics.com; 16-17: Seapics.com; 19 top left: Lundgren/Nature
Picture Library/Getty Images; 19 top right: OceanBodhi/iStockphoto; 19 bottom left: paulbcowell/iStockphoto; 19 bottom right:
Tobias Bernhard Raff/Biosphoto/Minden Pictures; 20-21: Buiten-Beeld/Alamy Images; 23: Laura Morse/IWC; 24-25: China
Photos/Getty Images; 26-27: Ye Maolin - CNImaging/Newscom; 28-29: Anne Rippy/Getty Images; 31: T Stitch/DeAgostini
Picture Library/Getty Images; 32-33: Bill Perry/Shutterstock; 34-35: Tatiana Grozetskaya/Shutterstock; 37: Seapics.com;
38-39 left: Rich Carey/Shutterstock; 39 right: John Keeble/Getty Images; 40-41: Darryl Dyck/The Canadian Press/AP Images;
42 bottom: GlobalP/iStockphoto; 42 center: Franco Banfi/Getty Images; 42 top left: Masa Ushioda/age fotostock; 42 top
right: Bill Curtsinger/Getty Images; 43 bottom left: Potapov Alexander/Shutterstock; 43 bottom right: Hiroya Minakuchi/Minden
Pictures; 43 top center: Miles Away Photography/Shutterstock; 43 top right: Richard Ellis/Getty Images; 43 top left: Jelger
Herder/Buiten-beeld/Minden Pictures.

Maps by Jim McMahon.

Table of Contents

Fact File: Porpoises

World Distribution
Coastal areas around the world

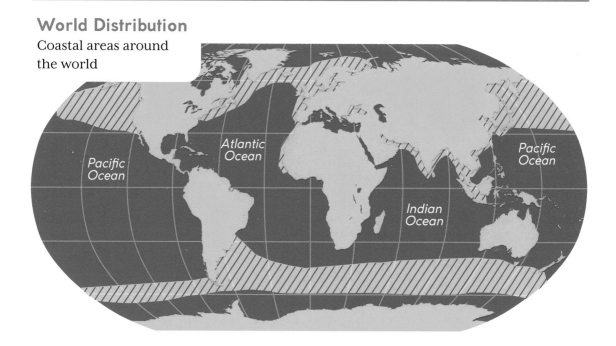

Pacific Ocean

Atlantic Ocean

Pacific Ocean

Indian Ocean

Population Status
Vulnerable or endangered, depending on species

Habitats
Mostly oceans; some rivers, lakes, and estuaries

Habits
Live in the water; communicate with high-pitched noises

Diet
Fish and other seafood

Distinctive Features
Smooth, rubbery, stout body with flippers, a dorsal fin, and a fluked tail; a small snout

Fast Fact
The name porpoise comes from the Latin *porcus*, for "pig."

Average Length

Dall's

6 ft. (2.4 m)

Vaquita

5 ft. (1.5 m)

Porpoises

4 ft. 6 in. (1.4 m)

Human (age 10)

Taxonomy

CLASS
Mammalia (mammals)

ORDER
Cetacea (marine)

FAMILY
Phocoenidae (porpoises, not the same as dolphins)

GENUS & SPECIES
- *Neophocaena asia orientalis* (finless porpoise)
- *Phocoena dioptrica* (spectacled porpoise)
- *Phocoena phocena* (common porpoise/ harbor porpoise)
- *Phocoena sinus* (Gulf of California harbor porpoise, vaquita porpoise)
- *Phocoena spinipinnis* (black porpoise, Burmeister's porpoise)
- *Phocoenoides dalli* (Dall's porpoise, True's porpoise)

CHAPTER 1

Endangered Porpoises

Pfffff! A spray of water shoots into the air. A small fin breaks the surface of the ocean, and there's a flash of a dark, sleek body beneath. It's a porpoise!

In salty oceans and in freshwater lakes and rivers all over the world, porpoises streak gracefully through the water. But these amazing creatures are getting harder to find. Water pollution, noise pollution, and illegal fishing have made certain porpoises **vulnerable** or **endangered** animals. For example, scientists think there are only about 30 vaquita porpoises left in the whole world. Without quick action, this animal could become **extinct**.

Porpoises are **mammals**, just like humans. They belong to a group of marine mammals called cetaceans (from a Greek word meaning "large sea creature").

▶ Porpoises are shy, but sometimes they can be spotted following boats.

Around the World

There are six different porpoise species. Different kinds of porpoises live in different habitats. Most porpoises prefer oceans, where they swim in the shallow waters near the coasts. But some species live in freshwater lakes and rivers. Others live in estuaries, the mouths of rivers, where the waters flow into the ocean.

Some species, like harbor porpoises, are common. They can be found in coastal areas along the Atlantic and Pacific Oceans and the Black Sea. Other types of porpoises are rare. The finless porpoises that live in China's Yangtze River are close to extinction.

◀ Harbor porpoises are the most plentiful species of porpoise, so scientists know the most about them.

Super Swimmers

Porpoises may come in different sizes and live in different places, but they have most things in common. A porpoise's body is perfectly adapted for swimming.

The porpoise has two flippers in front for steering. It has a wide, flat tail, called a fluke, that moves up and down. It propels the animal through the water.

A thick layer of fat, called blubber, keeps the porpoise's body warm in cold water. This super swimmer has a jellylike material in its eyes that keeps water from causing irritation. This is especially important in the salty ocean.

Though porpoises live underwater, they are mammals. So they breathe air. Instead of gills, as fish have, a porpoise has a blowhole. A porpoise swims to the water's surface approximately every 30 seconds to breathe. It must keep its blowhole clear of water or it could drown.

The vaquita is the smallest porpoise. It grows to about 5 feet (1.5 meters) long and weighs up to 120 pounds (54.4 kilograms). The Dall's porpoise is the largest. It can grow to up to 8 ft. (2.4 m) long and weigh up to 480 lb. (217.7 kg). The other species fall somewhere in between.

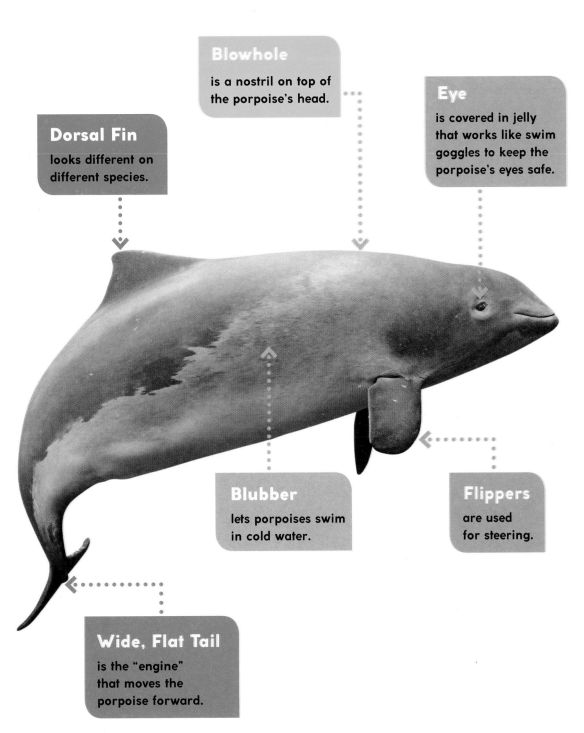

Dorsal Fin
looks different on different species.

Blowhole
is a nostril on top of the porpoise's head.

Eye
is covered in jelly that works like swim goggles to keep the porpoise's eyes safe.

Blubber
lets porpoises swim in cold water.

Flippers
are used for steering.

Wide, Flat Tail
is the "engine" that moves the porpoise forward.

11

Dolphin or Porpoise?

Many people confuse porpoises and dolphins. Some people even think they are the same animal. Dolphins are cetaceans, too. But they are not the same as porpoises. So how can you tell them apart?

Porpoises are small and roundish, and most species have a triangle-shaped dorsal fin. Dolphins are longer and leaner, with a curving dorsal fin. Porpoises can't turn their heads, the way dolphins can. That's because porpoises' necks are fused to their bodies, so they can swim quickly without their heads wobbling. Porpoise snouts are short and blunt. Dolphin snouts are longer and more beaklike. And dolphins have much pointier teeth. Dolphins are noisy and playful. Most porpoises are shy and quiet. That's why scientists know far less about these animals.

How are the two animals the same? They are both really smart!

◀ Bottlenose dolphins are known for their playful acrobatics.

CHAPTER 2

Water World

Staying safe in a watery habitat is not always easy! Since porpoises have to surface regularly in order to breathe, they can never fall completely asleep. If they did, they would drown. Scientists have discovered that porpoises sleep with only one side of their brain at a time. That way, they are awake enough to remember to surface when they need to. This is called "conscious breathing." They also sleep with one eye open at all times.

These survival techniques also help porpoises avoid predators. Orcas and sharks are their main threats. That's one reason porpoises prefer shallow coastal waters. Orcas and sharks don't often visit there.

Nevertheless, porpoises are always on the lookout for danger. Their eyesight is excellent. Large pupils help them see in deep, dark water. Porpoises can also close their eyes to tiny slits. This helps them see in bright light.

▶ An orca throws a Dall's porpoise in the air before killing it.

How Porpoises Move

Most mammals, including humans, are furry. But marine mammals have little or no hair on their bodies. If you ever have a chance to touch the skin of a porpoise, you will notice how rubbery it is. That smooth skin is important to their survival. It helps them glide easily and quickly through the water. Some porpoise species can swim at especially high speeds. Dall's porpoises have been timed going 35 miles per hour (56.3 kilometers per hour). That's quite a bit faster than the fastest person has ever run.

Dall's porpoises also dive the deepest. They can dive up to 1,640 ft. (546.7 m) deep and stay underwater for a few minutes at a time. They do this to hide from predators and to find food. Usually, however, porpoises stay near the surface to make breathing easier.

◀ When a Dall's porpoise reaches top speed, it makes a big splash of water called a "rooster tail."

What's for Lunch?

Porpoises feed mostly on fish, squid, and other seafood. They use their teeth to catch their prey, but they don't chew it. Instead, they swallow it whole, head first. That makes the food less likely to get stuck going down.

Porpoises prefer some tastes to others, so it seems clear they have a sense of taste. They *don't* have a sense of smell, though, as far as researchers can tell. Scientists are still studying and learning about porpoises' eating habits.

Porpoises eat many times throughout the day. That's because they have less blubber on their bodies than other marine mammals do. Porpoises need lots of food to keep their energy up and to stay warm in cold water.

▶ Porpoises are carnivores that eat a varied diet. It is made up of these sea creatures as well as many others.

Fast Fact
Porpoises (whose ears are inside their skulls) have great hearing.

Cod

Octopus

Mackerel

Squid

▶ Porpoises love to eat non-spiny fish such as cod.

▶ Its tender meat makes the ink-powered octopus a favorite prey.

▶ A big school of fish like mackerel is a feast for a porpoise.

▶ Porpoises around the world enjoy munching on this eight-armed mollusk.

How Porpoises Communicate

Porpoises do communicate with one another. But you will probably never hear most porpoise sounds. That's because they make very high-pitched noises that humans can't hear. Like bats and several other kinds of animals, porpoises use echolocation to communicate.

Animals that use echolocation call out. Then they wait for those calls to bounce off the things around them and echo back. That lets the animal discover the shape of the object, what it is, and where it's located. Porpoises use echolocation to find food and to keep track of other animals. They also use it to watch out for danger and to find their way around the dark parts of the ocean. Sound travels more than four times as fast and as far through water as through air. That makes it easier for porpoises to hear and communicate with each other.

Some porpoises also make clicking and puffing noises, usually to socialize with other porpoises. They can communicate with body language, too—by touching and head-butting.

◀ A bulge in the porpoise's forehead, called a melon, helps with echolocation.

CHAPTER 3

The All-Porpoise Life

One of the most vital jobs of female porpoises is to have babies. By the time they are between three and five years old, they are ready to become mothers. Male porpoises, called bulls, may mate with many females each year. But female porpoises, called sows, mate with a bull only once every few years. In between, they take care of the babies they give birth to.

Human babies grow inside their mothers for nine months. The **gestation** time for porpoises is a bit longer, about 10 to 11 months. The mother doesn't really have room in her body for more than one baby at a time. The low birth rate of porpoises—only one baby every few years—is one reason it's so important to protect these animals. It takes a long time for the population to grow.

▶ Spectacled porpoises give birth in spring and summer.

Oh, Baby!

Late spring is the beginning of baby season for porpoises. Like all mammals, babies are born live from their mother's body, rather than from eggs. The babies are called calves, or sometimes pups, and they are born completely underwater. A newborn porpoise emerges from its mother tail first, blowhole last. That protects the blowhole from filling with water and causing the calf to drown. Calves can swim from the moment they are born. They swim right to the surface to take their first breath.

Twin porpoises are very rare. In 2017, some Dutch fishermen found a two-headed harbor porpoise that had died and been caught in their net. It was a newborn **conjoined twin** porpoise. Scientists had never seen a case like that before.

◀ A rare, bred-in-captivity baby finless porpoise joins its mother and brother at the Chinese Academy of Sciences.

Ready, Set, Squirt!

As with all mammals, the first food for a porpoise calf is its mother's milk. Feeding takes place underwater. But the calf's mouth isn't the right shape to **nurse** directly from its mother, the way human babies do. The porpoise can't make an airtight, watertight seal with its mouth. Instead, a porpoise mother stays very close to her baby and *squirts* the milk into the calf's mouth.

Calves nurse for one to two years. Their mothers stay close by and care for them. Scientists believe that the father is not involved in raising the young. After young porpoises are **weaned**, they are ready to be on their own. They begin to eat fish and seafood. Soon they will look for mates and become parents themselves.

▶ Porpoise milk is thick, almost like a creamy milk shake!

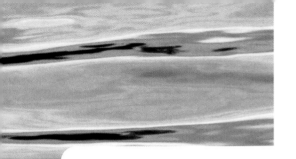

Fast Fact
Finless porpoises are the only species that do fairly well in captivity.

Porpoises in a Pod

Porpoises often live alone. Some species, such as harbor porpoises and Dall's porpoises, live in small social groups called pods. Porpoise pods can range in size from just two to 20 animals in each. Once in a while, many pods come together and form a much larger group in order to hunt and eat.

Porpoises don't **migrate** as much as some other animals. However, they do travel small distances to move to warmer waters or to reach more plentiful food supplies.

Porpoises have the shortest **lifespan** of all cetaceans. They live for about 10 to 20 years in the wild. Since catching porpoises to study in **captivity** has not been successful, scientists don't know as much as they would like to about these mysterious marine mammals.

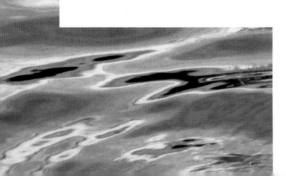

◄ When porpoises stay close to the surface, alternating between high-speed swimming and long jumps, it's called porpoising.

CHAPTER 4

All in the Cetacean Family

Would you believe that prehistoric relatives of the porpoise lived on land? Scientists have found cetacean remains from 53 million years ago. These porpoise **ancestors** were probably furry, four-legged creatures that hunted for fish at the water's edge.

As time went on, these ancient land animals spent more and more time in the water. Over millions of years, their front legs turned into flippers, and they lost their back legs completely. Their tails got wider and finally became the flukes that porpoises have today. Their bodies grew blubber to protect them in the water. And their nostrils moved to the top of their heads—becoming blowholes—so they could continue to breathe fresh air.

▶ **This artwork shows prehistoric and modern marine mammals.** *Eurhinodelphis* (second from bottom left) is related to porpoises.

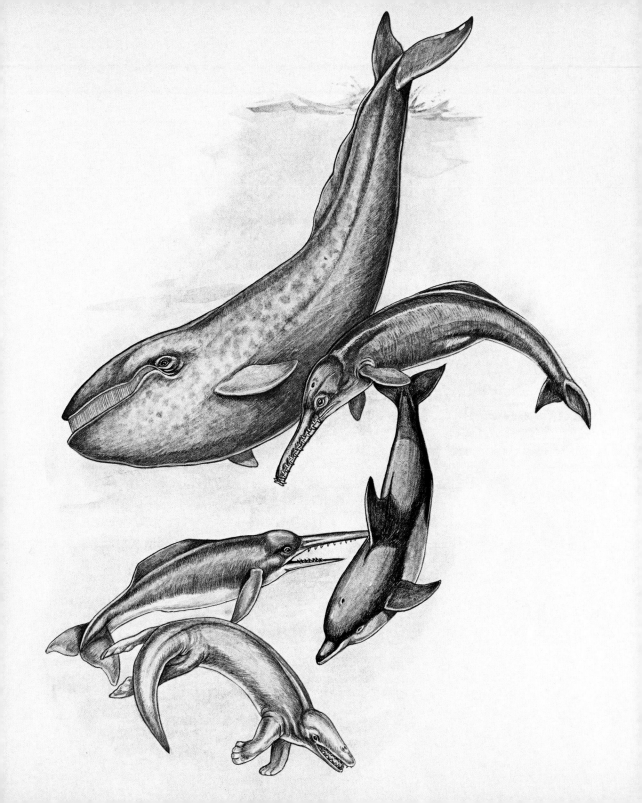

That's Fishy!

In ancient times, people didn't know porpoises were mammals. They thought they were fish. Aristotle, a Greek scientist and **philosopher** who lived in the fourth century B.C.E., studied them more closely. He observed their bodies and the way they moved, breathed, and lived. He realized that they were very different from fish.

But the ancient Greeks and Romans still believed that dolphins and porpoises were the same species. In Greek mythology, dolphins (and porpoises) were the messengers of Poseidon, the god of the seas. And Roman art often showed Cupid, the god of love, riding on their backs.

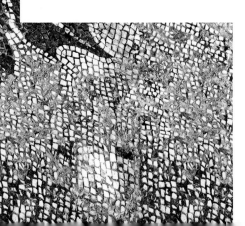

▶ In this Roman mosaic, Cupid rides on the back of a porpoise.

Hip, Hippo, Hooray!

Like all mammals, cetaceans—porpoises, dolphins, and toothed whales—are warm-blooded. That means they can make their own body heat and maintain their body temperature when their surroundings are cold. That is important for porpoises, that may live where the water is chilly. Being mammals also means they breathe air through their lungs.

Not *all* cetacean relatives live in the water, however. The closest living relative to this family is the hippopotamus. Like porpoises, hippos are almost hairless. And although hippos live on land, they spend a lot of time in the water. The common ancestor of hippos and cetaceans was a four-footed, partly **aquatic** mammal that lived many millions of years ago. As time went on, the hippos **evolved** in one direction and the cetaceans in another.

▶ Scientists once thought hippos were more closely related to pigs. (They're not!)

34

Dangerous Times

The number of porpoises in the world is falling. One threat that endangers these creatures is hunting. In Japan, people eat Dall's porpoise meat. Other people use porpoise blubber for products such as soap, candlewax, and makeup.

But an even bigger threat to porpoises is fishing. Porpoises are often caught in nets that fishermen have set to catch other kinds of fish. Porpoises caught in these nets usually drown because they can't come up for air.

New laws are being passed to protect the porpoises. The most harmful ways of fishing are now illegal. New kinds of nets are being used that are kinder to porpoises. Some make pinging noises to warn marine mammals away from dangerous netting. Weak links may be built into netting, allowing larger animals to break free if they're tangled. People who don't obey the strict new laws have to pay big fines. They may even go to jail.

▶ This Dall's porpoise drowned when it became trapped in a fishing net.

▲ More than 8 million tons of plastic end up in our oceans every year.

Dirty Waters

Pollution is an even bigger threat to porpoises. Polluted water harms all creatures that live in it. More factories are being built along China's Yangtze River and lakes. The factories empty **sewage** into the water and endanger the finless porpoises that live there. Porpoises may also eat plastic bags and other trash, which can kill them.

Noise pollution in the world's oceans also causes problems. Boats and ships not only pollute the water with oil but also make loud noises, which confuse porpoises. The noises make it hard for the animals to use echolocation to **navigate** and hunt for food. Sometimes they lose their way and are stranded on beaches.

How to Help a Stranded Porpoise

Be careful—remember that these are wild animals! Get help from a grownup to:

· Call the nearest aquatic park or animal rescue organization.
· Use a beach umbrella or a water-soaked towel to protect the porpoise's eyes.
· Keep the porpoise's blowhole clear of water.
· Do not attempt to move the porpoise before rescue workers arrive.

Helping to Save the Porpoise

For more than 60 years, harbor porpoises were absent from California's San Francisco Bay. Now they have returned. That's exciting news for **conservationists**.

All over the world, people are working hard to save porpoises. The entire Indian Ocean and the waters around Antarctica have been made **sanctuaries** for porpoises, dolphins, and whales. That means no hunting is allowed. Other safe areas have also been suggested. In 2016, the presidents of Mexico and the United States announced they would cooperate on laws to help the endangered vaquita porpoise. The Chinese government is taking steps to save finless porpoises, and is moving some of them to protected areas.

The more scientists know about porpoises, the easier it will be to come up with ways to protect them. Hopefully, with the information scientists provide and with hard work and people who care, these amazing creatures will continue to live and thrive in the oceans, lakes, and rivers of the world.

▶ This harbor porpoise was rescued after being stranded on a beach.

Porpoise Family Tree

Porpoises are mammals. Mammals are warm-blooded animals that have hair or fur and usually give birth to live babies; female mammals produce milk to feed their young. Mammals comprise more than 5,000 species. They all share a common ancestor that lived 100 million years ago. This diagram shows how porpoises are related to some other mammals and, specifically, to other types of mammals that live in water, such as whales, dolphins, and narwhals. The closer together two animals are on the tree, the more similar they are.

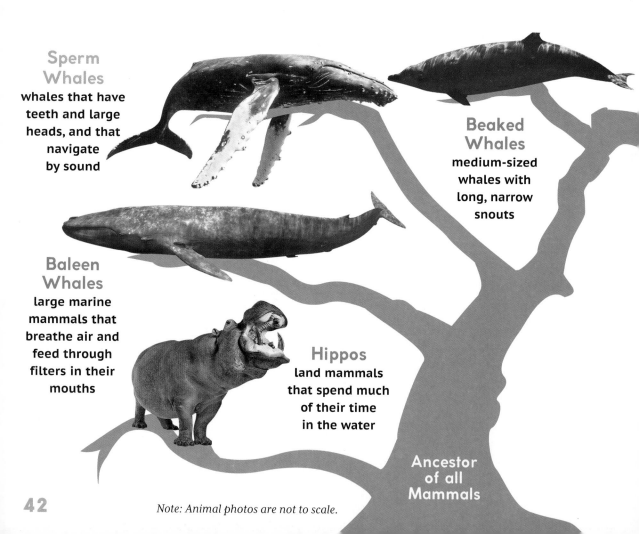

Sperm Whales
whales that have teeth and large heads, and that navigate by sound

Beaked Whales
medium-sized whales with long, narrow snouts

Baleen Whales
large marine mammals that breathe air and feed through filters in their mouths

Hippos
land mammals that spend much of their time in the water

Ancestor of all Mammals

Note: Animal photos are not to scale.

Beluga Whales

small-toothed whales with white skin and no dorsal fin

Narwhals

small whales with a tooth that grows into a long tusk

Porpoises

small marine mammals with short snouts and rounded bodies

Oceanic Dolphins

small to medium-sized marine mammals with teeth and dorsal fins

Words to Know

A.......... **adapted** *(ad-ap-TED)* changed or improved to better fit into one's environment

ancestors *(ANN-sess-tuhrs)* family members who lived long ago

aquatic *(uh-KWAT-ik)* living or growing in water

C.......... **captivity** *(kap-TIV-i-tee)* the condition of living in the care of people

conjoined twin *(kun-JOYND twin)* two babies who are joined together and share some parts of their bodies

conservationists *(kahn-sur-VAY-shun-ists)* people who protect valuable things, especially forests, wildlife, or natural resources

E.......... **echolocation** *(EK-oh-loh-KAY-shuhn)* a way of locating distant or invisible objects using sound waves reflected back to the sender from the objects

endangered *(en-DAYN-juhrd)* a plant or animal that is in danger of becoming extinct, usually because of human activity

evolved *(i-VAHLVD)* changed slowly and naturally over time

extinct *(ik-STINGKT)* no longer found alive

F.......... **fused** *(FYOOZD)* joined or grown together

G.......... **gestation** *(jeh-STAY-shuhn)* the period of time a baby grows and develops in its mother's body

H.......... **habitats** *(HAB-i-tats)* the places where an animal or plant is usually found

L.......... **lifespan** *(LIFE-span)* the period of time a person, an animal, a plant, or an object is expected to live or last

M.......... **mammals** *(MAM-uhlz)* warm-blooded animals that have hair or fur and usually give birth to live babies; female mammals produce milk to feed their young

migrate *(MYE-grate)* to move to another area or climate at a particular time of year

N.......... **navigate** *(NAV-i-gate)* to find where you are and where you need to go

nurse *(NURS)* to drink milk from a breast

P.......... **philosopher** *(fuh-LAH-suh-fur)* a person who studies ideas about life and seeks knowledge, truth, and wisdom

predators *(PRED-uh-tuhrs)* animals that live by hunting other animals for food

prey *(PRAY)* an animal that is hunted by another animal for food

S.......... **sanctuaries** *(SANGK-choo-er-eez)* natural areas where birds or animals are protected from hunters

sewage *(SOO-ij)* liquid and solid waste that is carried off by sewers and drains

species *(SPEE-sheez)* one of the groups into which animals and plants are divided; members of the same species can mate and have offspring

V.......... **vulnerable** *(VUHL-nur-uh-buhl)* a species that is facing threats and is likely to become endangered

W.......... **weaned** *(WEEND)* when a baby has stopped drinking its mother's milk and eats other foods instead

Find Out More

BOOKS

- Carwardine, Mark, illustrated by Camm, Martin. *Whales, Dolphins, and Porpoises*. New York: Dorling Kindersley Publishing, 2002.
- Hoyt, Erich. *Encyclopedia of Whales, Dolphins, and Porpoises*. Ontario, Canada: Firefly Books, 2017.
- Ryndak, Rob. *Dolphin or Porpoise?* New York: Gareth Stevens Publishing, 2016.

WEB PAGES

- www.porpoise.org/about-porpoises

  Information about the different species is presented by the Porpoise Conservation Society.
- www.worldwildlife.org/species/dolphins-and-porpoises

  Facts, photos, and videos from the World Wildlife Fund.
- www.whales.org

  Information on a large number of cetaceans from Whale and Dolphin Conservation.

Facts for Now

Visit this Scholastic Web site for more information on porpoises: **www.factsfornow.scholastic.com** Enter the keyword Porpoises

Index

Index *(continued)*

About the Author

Jodie Shepherd is the author of dozens of children's books and is an editor at Sesame Workshop. On a recent trip to Norway, she was thrilled to spot some harbor porpoises. She loves all animals, except maybe mosquitoes.